RURAL

ARCHITECTURE

IN THE

CHINESE

TASTE

WILLIAM AND JOHN HALFPENNY

BENJAMIN BLOM   New York/London 1968

Reprinted from the Third Edition, London 1755

Reprinted 1968 by Benjamin Blom, Inc., Bronx, N.Y. 10452
and 56 Doughty Street, London, W.C. 1

Library of Congress Catalog Card Number

Printed in the United States of America

Rural Architecture
in the
Chinese Taste,

Being Designs Entirely New

for the Decoration of

Gardens, Parks, Forrests, Insides of Houses, &c.

on Sixty Copper Plates

with full Instructions for Workmen

ALSO

A near Estimate of the Charge,
and Hints where proper to be Erected.

the Whole Invented & Drawn by

Will.ᵐ & Jn.ⁿ Halfpenny, Architects.

The 3ᵈ Edition.

With the Addition of 4 Plates in Quarto, of Roofs for
Chinese & Indian Temples, the manner of fixing
their Ornaments, Covering and carrying off the
Water, their Cornices with the several Members
adjusted to regular Proportion

LONDON, 1755.

Printed for Robt. Sayer, at the Golden Buck, opposite
Fetter Lane, Fleetstreet

THE

PREFACE

MY first Essays of CHINESE Architecture being so well receiv'd by the Publick, has encouraged me to add many Improvements thereto; and to render that Taste of Building more compleat, I have, with the Assistance of my Son, published this Second Part, hoping we have not only improved the former Sketches, but laid down several Objects in the Chinese Manner hitherto unknown, yet made easy to the meanest Capacity, by

WIL. and JOHN HALFPENNY.

THE

PREFACE.

THE *Art of designing Archi-tecture is not confined to any particular Taste or Country, more than jnstly observing a graceful Sym-metry, and an exact Proportion tho-rough the whole. And the* Chinese *Manner of Building being introduced here with Success, the few follow-ing Essays are an Attempt to rescue those agreeable Decorations from the many bad Consequences usually at-tending such slight Structures, when unskilfully erected : Which must often unavoidably happen at a Di-*

B   *stance*

The PREFACE.

stance from this Metropolis, without such Helps as, I flatter myself, the Workmen will here find laid down by,

Their Well-Wisher,

WIL. HALFPENNY.

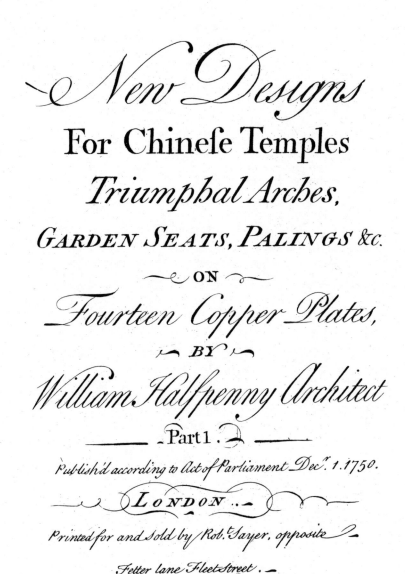

New Designs

For Chinese Temples

Triumphal Arches,

GARDEN SEATS, PALINGS &c.

ON

Fourteen Copper Plates,

BY

William Halfpenny Architect

Part 1.

Publish'd according to Act of Parliament Dec.r 1.1750.

LONDON

Printed for and sold by Rob.t Sayer. opposite

Fetter lane Fleet Street.

B O O K S

Printed for ROBERT SAYER,

MAP and PRINT-SELLER,

At the GOLDEN BUCK, oppofite FETTER-LANE, FLEET-STREET.

I.

THE firft and fecond Parts of Chinefe Architecture, being new Defigns of Plans and Elevations for Temples, Triumphal Arches, Garden Seats, Palings, Bridges, Obelifks, Terminis, &c. with full Inftructions to Workmen, annex'd to each particular Defign, a near Eftimate of their Charge and Hints, where, with moft Advantage, to be erected. The whole invented and drawn by *William* and *John Halfpenny*, Architects, Price 2s. 6d. each Part.

II.

Twenty new Defigns of Chinefe Lattice, and other Works for Stair-Cafes, Gates, Palings, Hatches, &c. on fix Folio Copper Plates; with full Inftructions annexed to the feveral Divifions, Scantlings, &c. thereby making the whole eafy to Workmen of every Capacity, by *William Halfpenny*, Architect, Price 2s.

III.

Twelve beautiful Defigns for farm Houfes, with their proper Offices and Eftimates of the whole, and every diftinct Building feparate, with the Meafurement and Value of each particular Article, adapted to the cuftomary Meafurements of moft Parts of *Englond*; but more particularly for the following Counties, *viz. Middlefex, Surrey, Effex, Kent, Suffex, Hampfhire, Hertfordfhire, Cambridgefhire, Berkfhire, Buckinghamfhire, Oxfordfhire, Wiltfhire, Gloucefterfhire,* and *Somerfet-fhire;* by *William Halfpenny,* Architect, Price 6s.

IV.

A new and compleat Syftem of Architecture, delineated in a Variety of Plans and Elevations of Defigns for convenient and decorated Houfes; together with Offices and Out-buildings proportioned thereto, and appropriated to the feveral Ufes and Situations required. Prefixed to thefe are ten different Sorts of Piers, with Gates of various Compofitions fuitable to the fame, intended for Entrances to Courts, Gardens, &c. As alfo new architectodic Rules for drawing the Members in all Kinds and Proportions of the Orders, with Explanations thereto in common Prefs Work, 8s.

Designs

Plate 2.

A Chinese Single brac'd Paling

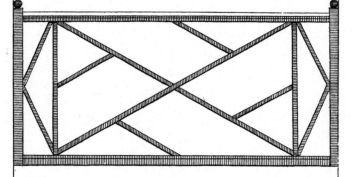

A Chinese Double brac'd Paling

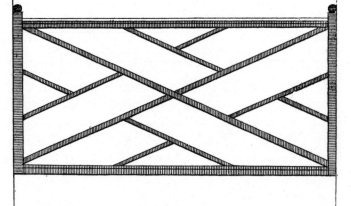

Plate 3.

A Chinese Acute angular Paleing

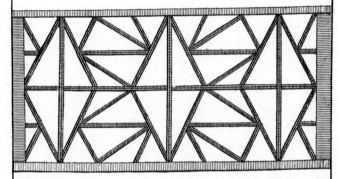

A Chinese Obtuse & Diamond Paleing.

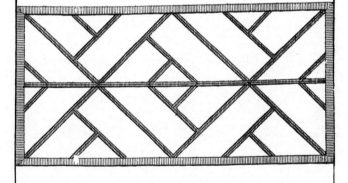

Plate 4.

A Chinese half diamond brac'd Paling.

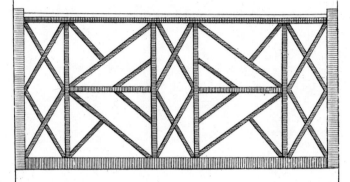

A Chinese diamond brac'd Paling.

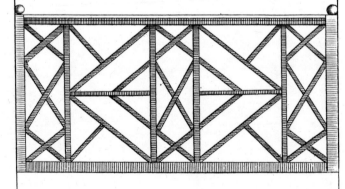

Plate 5.

A Chinese Hatch &c.

A Chinese Parallelogram Hatch &c.

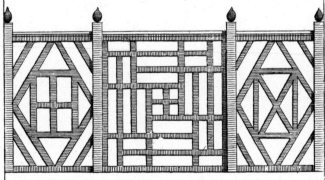

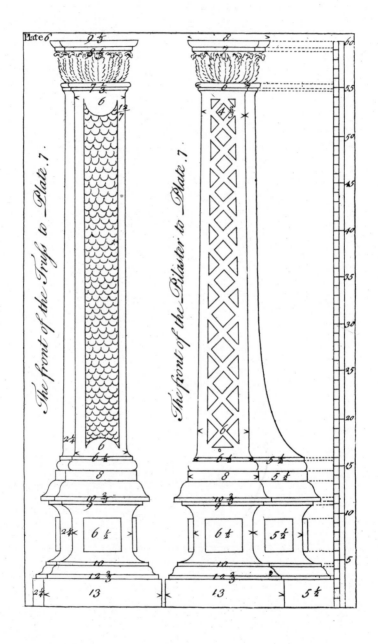

Plate 6

The front of the Trufs to *Plate 7*.

The front of the Pilaster to *Plate 7*.

Plate 7.

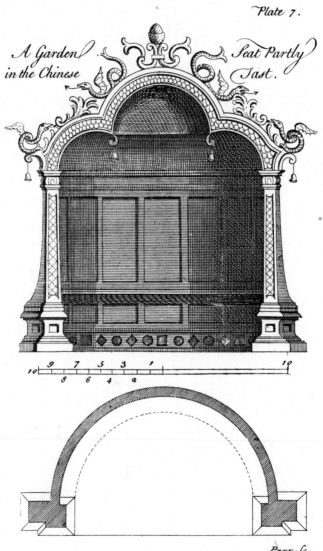

A Garden in the Chinese   *Seat Partly Tast.*

Parr Sc.

Plate 8.

A Chinese   *Alcove Seat*
Fronting   *Four Ways.*

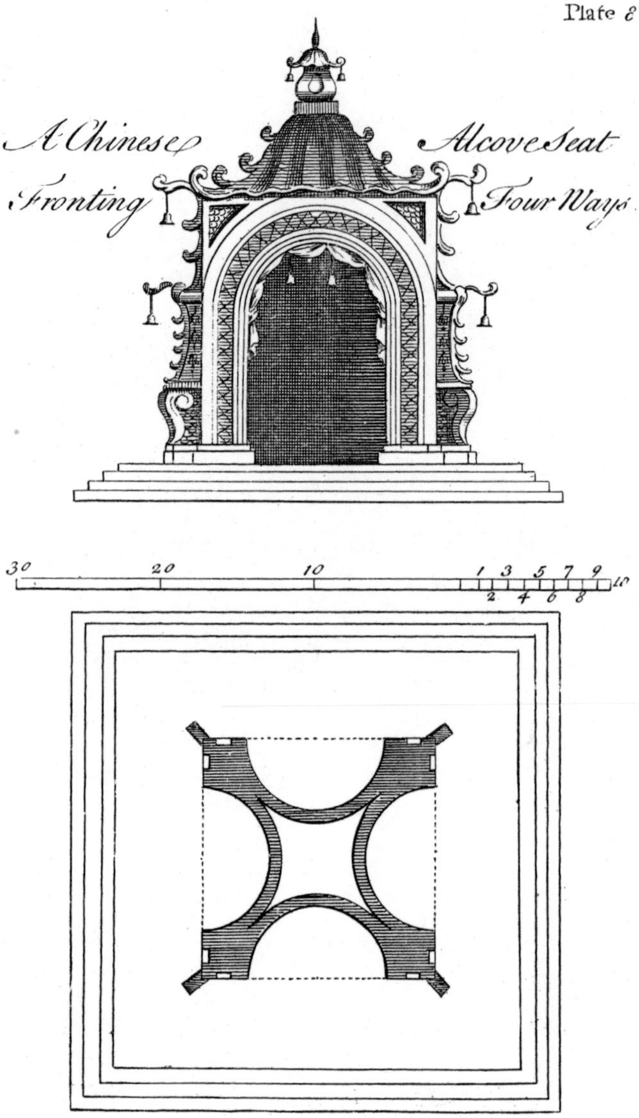

30   20   10   1 3 5 7 9
                               2 4 6 8 10

Plate 9.

A Temple in the Chinese Tast

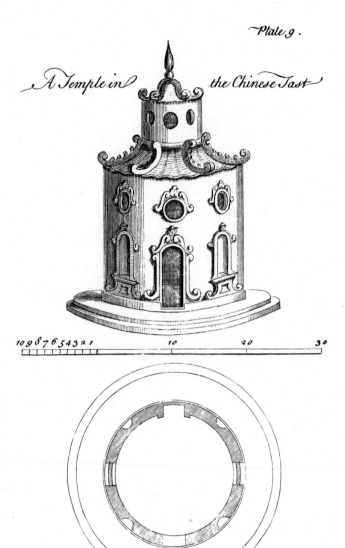

10 9 8 7 6 5 4 3 2 1   10   20   30

Parr Sc.

Plate 10.

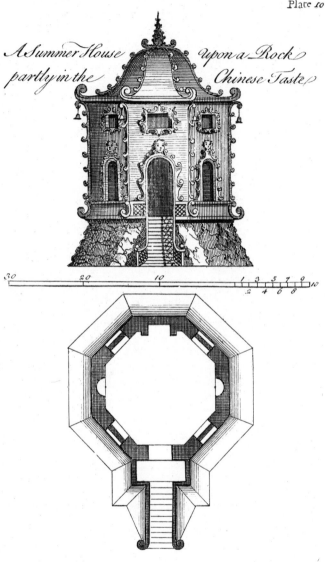

A Summer House upon a Rock partly in the Chinese Taste

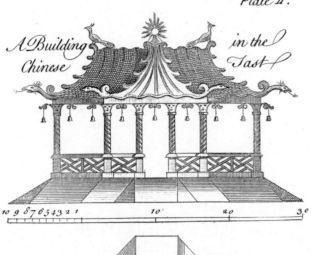

A Building in the
Chinese Tast

Parr Sc.

Plate 12.

A Chinese　　　Temple

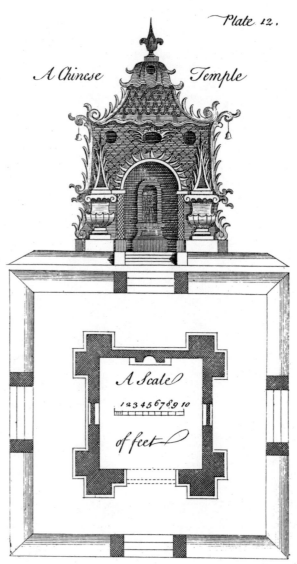

A Scale
1 2 3 4 5 6 7 8 9 10
of feet

Parr Sc.

Plate *13*.

A Banqueting House in the Chinese Taste

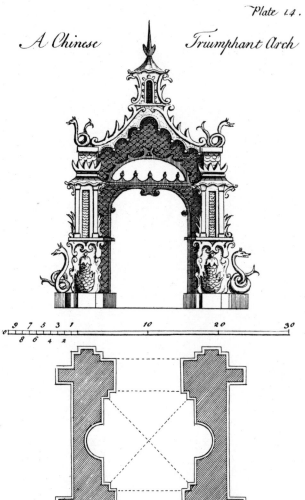

Plate 14.

A Chinese   Triumphant Arch

0 9 7 5 3 1   10   20   30
  8 6 4 2

Parr Sc.

PART I.

Of Rural Buildings in the Chinese Taſte, for Temples, Triumphal Arches, Garden Seats, Palings, &c.

PLATE I.
The Title.

PLATE II.

Shews two Sorts of Framing for Palings, Bridges, &c.

The firſt is term'd Single-brac'd Framing, each Bay containing ſeven Pieces of Bracing, as in the Example. The four Side Braces are not included.

The moſt methodical Manner in laying down the Lines for this Work, is to divide the Length into four equal Parts, and the Height into the ſame, by perpendicular and horizontal Lines, whoſe Interſections point out the Middle of every Mortiſe and Tenon ; but the Workman muſt obſerve in this, and all Works of this Kind, to ſet half the Width of an inſide Timber or Brace on the inward Edge of each of the out-ſide Timbers, as Poſts, Rails, or upright Bars, otherwiſe the Diviſion will not be equal.

N. B. *A Bay is underſtood by Carpenters to be the Meaſure from Middle to Middle of two Main-poſts.*

B 2   The

The second is term'd Double-braced Framing, whose Length must be divided into six equal Parts, and the Height into the same, by perpendicular and horizontal Lines, which will point out the Middle of every Mortise and Tenon, as beforeme ntioned.

PLATE III.

Contains two Bays of different Kinds; the first is term'd Acute Angular Paling, whose Length must be divided into eight equal Parts, and its Height into four, by perpendicular and horizontal Lines.

The second is termed Double-braced and Diamond Paling, whose Length must be divided into six equal Parts, and its Height into the same, by perpendicular and horizontal Lines.

PLATE IV.

Shews two different Bays of Paling; the first is termed Half-diamond braced Framing, whose Length must be divided into seven equal Parts, and its Height into four, by perpendicular and horizontal Lines.

The second is termed Whole Diamond braced Paling, which must be divided into the same Number of Parts as the foregoing.

PLATE V.

Containing two Hatches with a Bay on each Side; the first is termed a Diamond-Hatch, which is divided into two Diamonds, four Parallelograms, eight Acute and eight Right Angles, whose Width and Height is divided into two equal Parts, and the large Diamond first described. Its Sides must each be divided into three equal Parts, and Lines drawn parallel thereto, then describe the outward Braces from Angle to Angle.   The

The Bay on the Right is divided in the same Manner, except the Braces which divide the Parallelograms.

The Bay, on the Left, is divided into three equal Parts, high and wide, by perpendicular and horizontal Lines.

The second Figure is termed a Parallelogram Hatch, whose Heighth and Width must be divided, each into eight equal Parts, by perpendicular and horizontal Lines, and the Bays on the Sides each into four equal Parts wide, and four high.

PLATE VI.

Shews the Front and Profile of the Pilaster and Trufs, with their Pedestals to the Cove Seat. *Plate* 7. See their Proportions.

The whole Height is divided into 60 equal Parts, which gives the several Heights by the Help of horizontal dotted Lines from the Scale to the Object ; the Figures on the Members are so many of those 60 Parts. For Example, the Diameter of the Pilaster at the Base is 6, and under the Capital 4 $\frac{2}{3}$ of those Parts ; the Front of the Trufs is 6 at the Base, and 6 under the Capital; and so of all the other Members.

PLATE VII.

Shews the Plan and Elevation of a double-coved Garden-Seat, supposed to be fixed at the Termination of a large Walk ; and its Width in the Clear is 17 Feet, and 14 Feet high from the Floor to the Foot of the lower Cove, and 22 high in Front ; the back Wall up to the Pitch

of

of the Roof may be built of Brick, or Timber filled with four Inch Brick ; and the Ornaments may be made of Wood, decorated in the *Chinese* Manner, with netted Work, &c. which may be executed for about 100 *l.*

PLATE VIII.

Reprefents a Building, in which is contained four cove Seats, and may be fitly fituated in the Center of a large Square or Lawn, (raifed above the common Surface by a Mount or Steps) about which are Woods or Plantations, with a grand Avenue from each Front. It may be built of Timber filled with four Inch Brick, and ftucco'd within and without. Above the Crown of the Coves may be made a Room, wherein Muficians may be fecreted, and play on foft Mufick to the agreeable Surprize of Strangers, the Performers going in by a fubterranean Paffage, and a broad Step Ladder between the Backs of the Seats, and lighted by fmall Windows in the Roof concealed from without. The Building may be executed for about 170 *l.* Steps not included.

PLATE IX.

Shews the Plan and Elevation of a circular Temple, proper to be built on an Eminence for a diftant Mark ; its Diameter, in the Clear, is 16 Feet ; the Cupola may be open to the Room, whofe Ceiling will be 26 Feet above the Floor, and a Cove made under the firft Roof, to finifh to a Colofs fixed to the Kerb, wherein the Cupola is framed. The Walls, up to the Pitch of the Roof, are fuppofed to be Brick or Stone,

2   and

and the Cupola Timber filled with four Inch Brick. The Ornaments about the Door and Windows carved in Stone, and thofe on the Roof of Timber. This Building may be executed for about 220 *l.*

PLATE X.

Reprefents the Plan and Elevation of an Octagon Summer-houfe, 14 Feet Diameter, and 14 Feet high from the Floor to the Cieling, elevated on an artificial Rock, in which a Cellar, or Grotto, may be made. The Walls may be Brick, Stone, or Timber, and the Ornaments cut in Stone or Wood, and the Rails of the Steps Lattice Work. This Building, not including the Rock, may be executed, in a good Manner, for about 230 *l.*

PLATE XI.

Shews the Plan and Elevation of an open Building; the Length extends in the Clear 26 Feet fix Inches, and its narroweft Widths 12 Feet, raifed on twifted Timber Pillars, and inclofed by Braced-Work Paling; it's fuppofed to be elevated above the common Surface on a large open Spot, where a Profpect is required every way, which may be built in a good Manner for about 240 *l.*

PLATE XII.

Shews the Plan and Elevation of a Temple 15 Feet in the Clear both ways, and 18 Feet from the Floor to the Cieling, under which is a Cove of three Feet. This Building is fuppofed

to

to be elevated on a small Rising (as in the Example) at the Termination of a grand Walk. The Walls may be built of Brick, or Timber filled with four Inch Brick stucco'd, and the Ornaments of Wood. This Building may be executed for about 280 *l.*

PLATE XIII.

The Plan and Elevation of a Banqueting-house, 18 Feet in the Clear both Ways, the Cupola open to the Room, whose Cieling will be 24 Feet above the Floor, and a Cove of three Feet six Inches under the first Roof, to finish at a Coloss fixed to the Kerb of the Roof, wherein the Cupola is framed. The Walls, up to the Pitch of the Roof, may be Brick, Stone, or Timber filled in with four Inch Bricks and stucco'd. This Building will be agreeably situated on a Grand Amphitheatre of green Slopes, or on a Terrass, *&c.* which may be executed in a good Manner for about 350 *l.*

PLATE XIV.

Shews the Plan and Elevation of a triumphal Arch, to be situated opposite the Front of a Dwelling-house, at the utmost Extent of a large Parterre, through which commences a Long-walk, inclosed by Woods or other rural Plantations. This Arch may be built in a good Manner for about 470 *l*

The End of the First Part.

NEW
DESIGNS

FOR

Chinese Bridges, Temples, Triumphal
Arches, Garden‑Seats, Palings,
Obelisks, Termini's, *&c.*

ON

FOURTEEN Copper Plates.

TOGETHER WITH

Full Instructions to Workmen
Annex'd to each particular Design;

A Near Estimate of their Charge,

And Hints *Where*, with most Advantage
to be *Erected*.

The Whole Invented and Drawn by

Will. and *John Halfpenny*, Architects.

PART II.

Published according to Act of Parliament, Feb. 1, 1751.

LONDON:

Printed for R. Sayer, Printseller, opposite *Fetter-
Lane, Fleet-Street.*

Pl. 15.

A Germany Seat in the Chinese Taste

W. Halfpenny inv.   *Parr Sculp*

Plate 16.

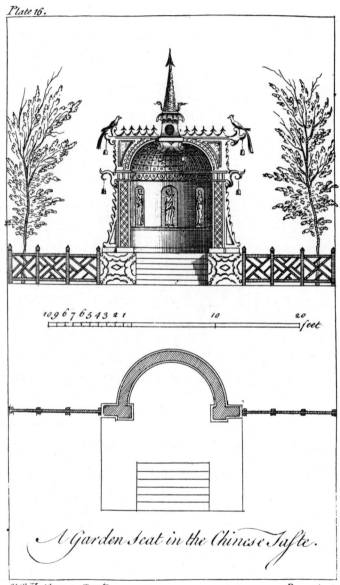

10 9 6 7 6 5 4 3 2 1   10   20
feet

A Garden Seat in the Chinese Taste.

Wm Halfpenny Inv.^t   Parr Sculp.

Plate 17.

An Open Temple or Garden Seat in the Chinese Taste.

10 9 6 7 6 5 4 3 2 1   10   20   feet
                                                                          30

W.ᵐ Halfpenny Inv.ᵗ   Parr Sculp

Plate 18.

A Temple in the Chinese Taste

10 9 8 7 6 5 4 3 2 1   10 feet

Wm Halfpenny Invt.   Parr Sc.

Plate 19.

A Building in the Chinese Taste.

10 9 8 7 6 5 4 3 2 1   10   20 feet

Wm Halfpenny Inv.^t   Parr Sc.

Plate 20.

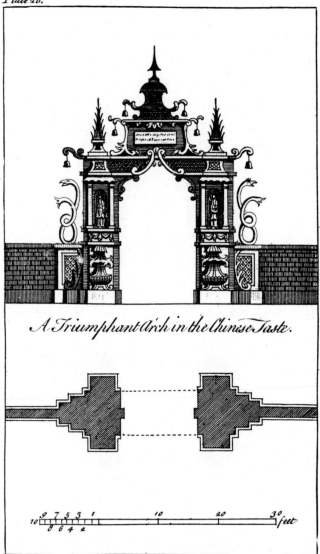

A Triumphant Arch in the Chinese Taste.

W.ᵐ Halfpenny Inv.ᵗ

Parr Sculp.

Plate 21.

A Termany in the Chinese Taste.

John Halfpenny Invt. delint.

inches 12 9 6 3   1   2   3   4   5 feet

Parr sculp

Plate 22.

A Termany in   the Chinese Taste.

inches
12 9 6 3   1   2   3   4   5   6   7 feet

John Halfpenny Inv.t et delin.   Parr sculp.

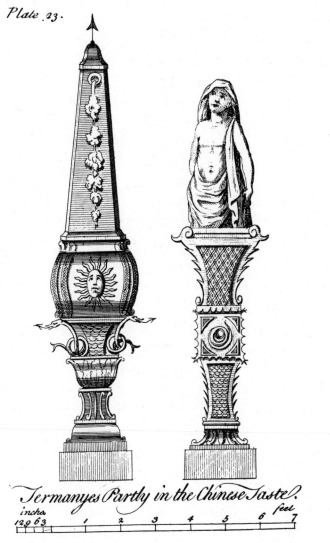

Plate 23.

Termanyes Partly in the Chinese Taste.

inches   feet

12 9 6 3   1   2   3   4   5   6   7

Iohn Halfpenny Invᵗ et delin.   *Parr sculp*

Plate 24.

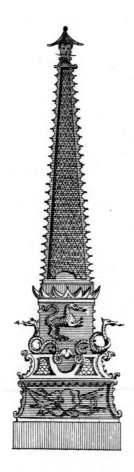

An Obulisk in the Chinese Taste.

Iohn Halfpenny Inv.ᵗ et delin.

PART II.

Containing Plans and Elevations for CHINESE BRIDGES, TEMPLES, TRIUMPHAL ARCHES, GARDEN-SEATS, OBELISKS, TERMINI's, &c.

PLATE XV.

THE Plan and Elevation of a Garden-Seat, compofed of Lattice Work, which may be covered with painted Canvas or otherwife. This Building will be moft properly fituated at the End of a Walk, or amidft rural Plantations, and may be genteely compleated for 45 *l.*

PLATE XVI.

The Plan and Elevation of a femi-circular cov'd Seat, on an Elevation three Feet fix Inches above the Surface, and afcended to by Steps of Stone, if nich'd (as in the Defign) the Walls muft be of Brick or Stone, or otherwife of Timber fill'd with four Inch Brick and ftucco'd. The Ornaments may be of Wood, &c. This Building is beft to be erected at the Extent of a Lawn, Avenue, or wide Walk. To be elegantly compleated for 130 *l.*

PLATE XVII.

The Plan and Elevation of a Temple erected on a Mount, and afcended to by an eafy Slope, the Walls may be Brick, Stone or Timber, filled with four inch Brick ; its Situation will be moft agreeable in a large Opening, encompafs'd with Woods

or

or rural Plantations, to which there is no other Paffage than ferpentine Walks, in order to caufe an agreeable Surprize at firft Sight ; and may be finifhed in the beft Manner for 115 *l.*

PLATE XVIII.

The Plan and Elevation of an open Temple, fupported by fquare Pillars, ornamented and enclofed by Lattice-Work ; to be fituated in the Center of a Grove or Wood, through which Walks are cut, fo will form an agreeable Profpect from feveral Places ; and may be built for 240 *l.*

PLATE XIX.

The Plan and Elevation of a Temple fourteen Feet by fourteen Feet in the Clear, the Cupola to be open to the Room, with a Cove under the firft Roof, which finifhes to a Colofs fixed to the Kerb of the Roof. The Cieling of the Cupola will be twenty Feet above the Floor ; the Walls may be made of Brick or Timber, fill'd with four inch Brick, and ftucco'd. This Building is to be fituated in the Center of a rural Plantation, with proper Walks or Avenues leading thereto ; it may be built for 200 *l.*

PLATE XX.

The Plan and Elevation of a triumphal Arch, being a proper Termination of a grand Avenue leading from a Gentleman's Seat to a Road or navigable River.

PLATE XXI, XXII, XXIII.

Reprefent the Elevations of Termini's for fhort Receffes in rural Plantations.

PLATE

PLATE XXIV.

The Elevation of an Obelisk 40 Feet high, proper to be situated at the Termination of a long Walk, or in the Center of a large Square, &c.
N. B. *Any of the foregoing Buildings may be either reduc'd or enlarged by altering the Scale.*

PLATE XXV.

Represents the Plan of a single truss'd Timber Bridge, whose Spand is 30 Feet and Width in the Clear 9 Feet. The Posts tend to the Center of the Curve, and the Floor of the Bridge, with the Rails, &c. answerable thereto; for the Length and Scantling of the Timbers see the Scale. This Bridge contains 380 Cube Feet of Timber.

PLATE XXVI.

Shews the Plan and Elevation of a double truss'd Timber Bridge, whose Spand between the Top of the Butment is 45 Feet, and the Width in the Clear 16 Feet, each Side is fram'd in five Bays, and the bearing Truss under the Middle of the Joist the same. The Curve next the Water is the Segment of a Circle, but the Floor of the Bridge with the Cornice which covers the Ends of the Joists, and Rails adjoining thereto and upper Rail are answerable to 'the Curve of a Cathanarian Arch, which is created by the swagging of a Chain, or they may be described by the Intersections of Lines*. The side Timbers and middle Pieces tend to the

* *N. B.* The practical Lines for these or any other Curves us'd in Building, may be seen in a Book, entitled *The Art of sound Building*, invented and published by me in the Year 1726, but are now found in several Volumes published by piratical Copiers extremely erroneous.

Center

Center of the lower Curve, and are groov'd and bolted together; fee their Plan A; the middle Pieces are taper, according to the fommering of the Arch, which may be drove in farther, in cafe of Slacknefs by the Butments fettling, or the Timber fhrinking, and may be drove out if a Repair fhould be wanting; either of the Bays may be taken out at Pleafure, by ftripping off the Cornice and fecuring the other Bays by Struts, while the Repairs are executing; for the Scantling of the Timbers fee the Scale. This Bridge contains 1012 Cube Feet of Timber.

PLATE XXVII.

Shews the Plan and Elevation of a fingle trufs'd Timber Bridge, whofe Spand is 60 Feet, and its Width in the Clear 16 Feet; the main Pofts are each in one Piece, and the Struts, which tend to the Center of the lower Curve, are two inch Oak Plank, each of one Length let through the main Timbers by Mortices, and faftened in by Pins; for the Length and Scantlings of the Timbers, fee the Scale. This Bridge contains 1040 Cube Feet of Timber.

The Pavillion placed on the Bridge is for the Conveniency of Angling, Mufick, &c. which may be fo contriv'd that it may be taken down or fet up at Pleafure.

PLATE XXVIII.

Shews the Plan and Elevation of a double trufs'd Timber Bridge, whofe Spand is 40 Feet, and its Width in the Clear 12 Feet, the main Pofts tend to the Center of the Curve, and are each in one Piece thro' both Truffes; for the Length and Scantling of the Timbers fee the Scale. This Bridge contains 831 Cube Feet of Timber.

F I N I S.

A single Injord Bridge — in the Chinese Taste.

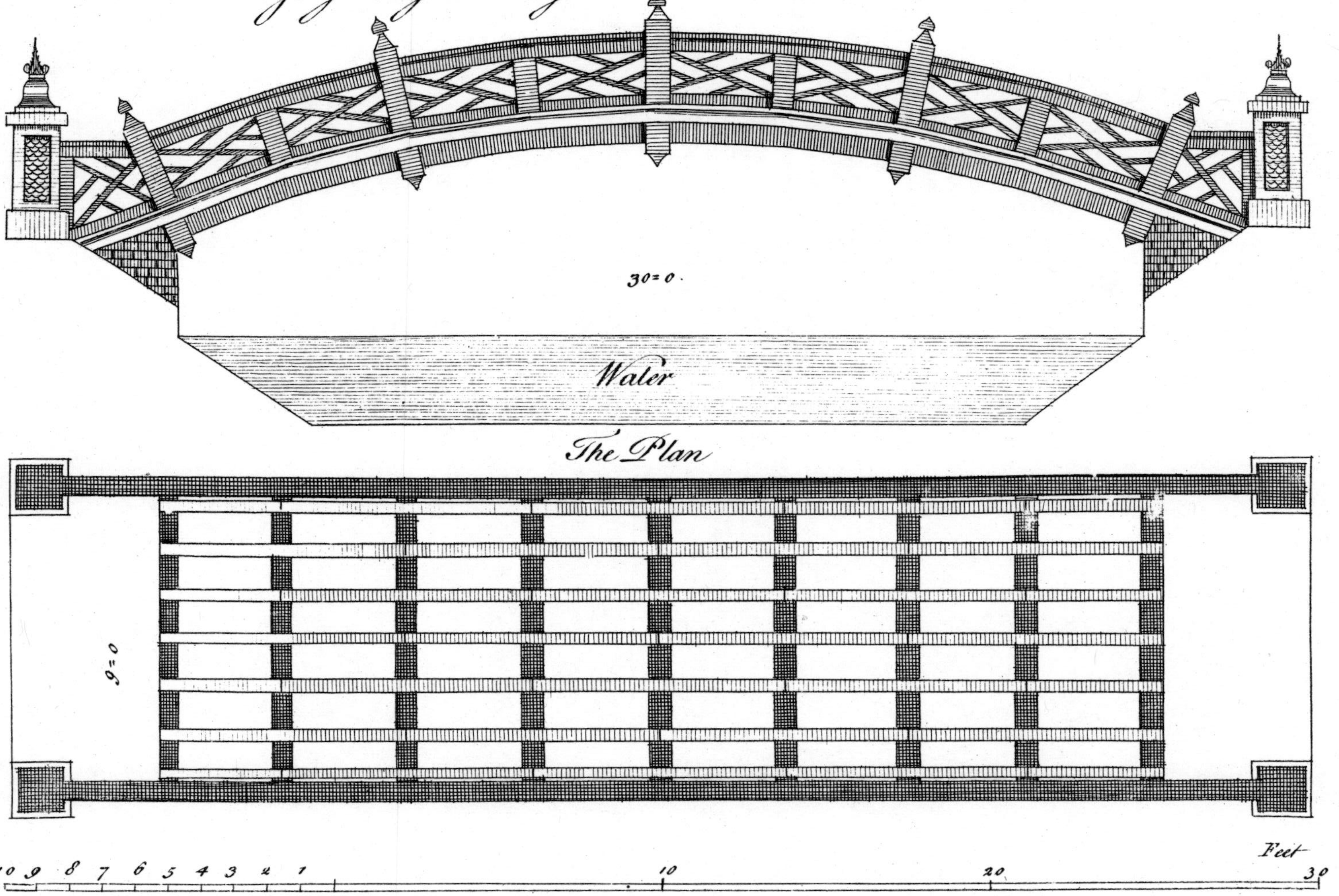

30=0.

Water

The Plan

0=6

Feet

I.m Halfpenny Invt et delin.

Parr sculp.

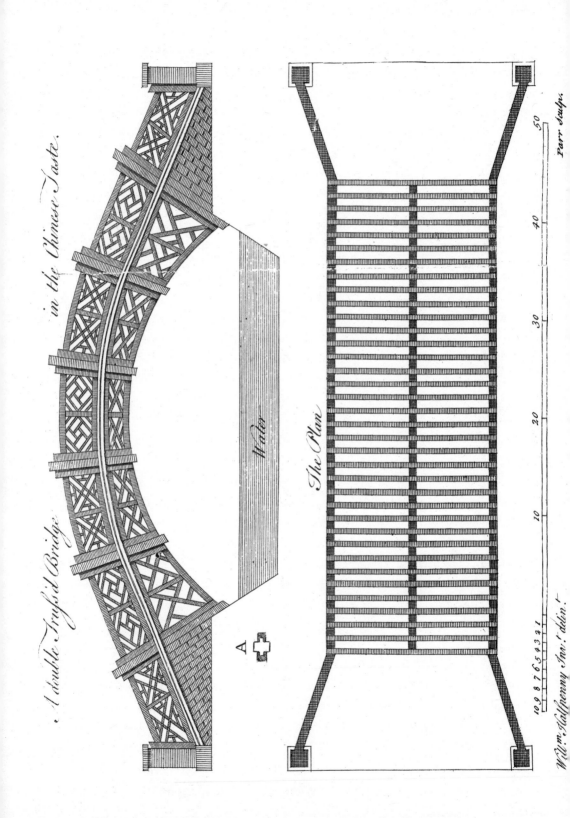

A double Trestil Bridge in the Chinese Taste.

Water

The Plan

A

10 9 8 7 6 5 4 3 2 1   10   20   30   40   50

Will.m Halfpenny Invt. delin.t

Parr sculp.

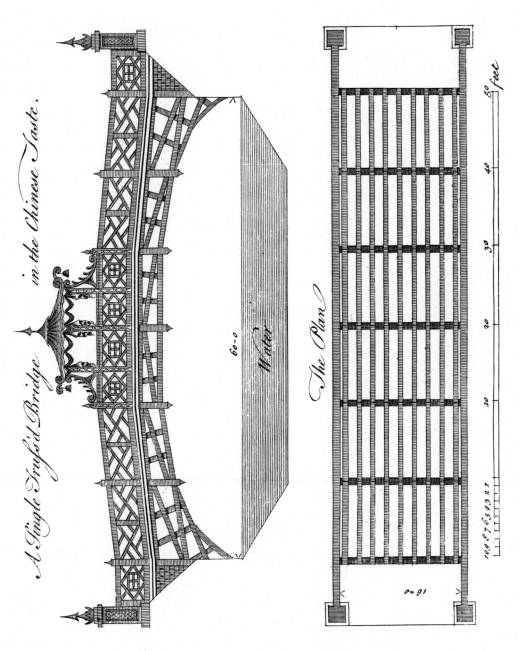

A Single Truss'd Bridge   *in the Chinese Taste.*

Water

60-0

The Plan

16=0

50 feet

10 9 8 7 6 5 4 3 2 1

W.ᵐ Halfpenny Inv.ᵗ et delin.

Parr Sculp.

Plate 28.

A double Truss'd Bridge   in the Chinese Taste.

40:0

Water

The Plan

30 feet

20

10

10 9 8 7 6 5 4 3 2 1

Plate 29

A Double Door in the Chinese Taste

Inches
12 6   1   2   3   4   5   6   7   8   9   feet

Plate 30

A Double Door in the Chinese Taste

inches
12 6   1   2   3   4   5   6   7   8   9   10   11 feet

Plate 31.

A Double Door in the Chinese Taste

Inches
12 6   1   2   3   4   5   6   7   8   9   feet

Plate 32

A Window in the Chinese Taste

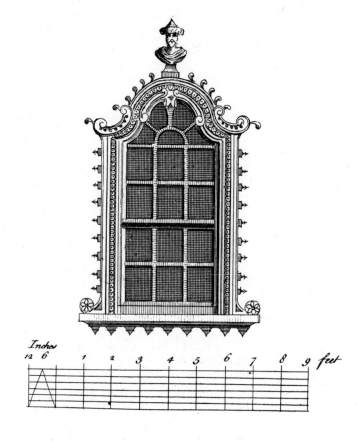

Inches
12 6   1   2   3   4   5   6   7   8   9 feet

Plate 33

A Window in the Chinese Taste

Inches
12 6 · · 1 · 2 · 3 · 4 · 5 · 6 · 7 · 8 · 9 feet

Plate 34.

A Window in the Chinese Taste

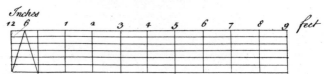

Inches
12 6   1   2   3   4   5   6   7   8   9 feet

Plate 35

A Peir in the Chinese Taste

inches
12 9 6 3   1   2   3   4   5   6   7   8   9   10   11 feet

A Peir or Pilaster in the Chinese Taste

inches
12 9 6 3   1   2   3   4   5   6   7   8   9   10   11   feet

Parr S.

Plate 37

A Peir or Pilaster in the Chinese Taste.

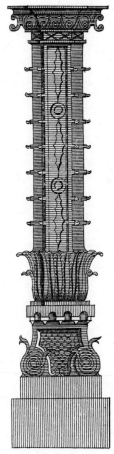

inches
12 9 6 3   1   2   3   4   5   6   7   8   9   feet

NEW

DESIGNS

FOR

Chinese Doors, Windows,
Piers, Pilasters, Garden
Seats, Green-Houses, Sum-
mer Houses, &c.

ON

SIXTEEN COPPER PLATES;

TOGETHER

With INSTRUCTIONS to Workmen,
Annexed to each particular Design;

The whole invented and drawn by

Will. and *John Halfpenny*, Architects.

PART III.

Published according to Act of Parliament, May 1st, 1751.

LONDON:

Printed for Robert Sayer, Map and Printseller, at
the Golden Buck, opposite *Fetter-Lane*, *Fleet-Street*.

PART III.

PLATE XXIX.

A Front Door decorated in the CHINESE manner, whose Heighth is equal to twice its Width; the Pilasters which bears the Arch are one fifth of the Door wide, and 8 Diameters high from the lower Line of the Plinth to the upper Line of the Chaptrel.

PLATE XXX.

Another Door of the same Proportion, whose Ornaments on each Side are equal to one fourth of the Width,

PLATE XXXI.

Another Door of the same Proportion, whose Pilasters on each Side are two ninths of the Door's Width, and 7 Diameters and two thirds high from the lower Line of the Plinth, to the upper Line of the Chaptrel.

PLATE

P L A T E XXXII.

A Window decorated in the CHINESE manner, whose Height, is equal to two Widths and one Sixth, and the Ornaments on each Side to one fifth of the Door.

P L A T E XXXIII.

Another Window of the same Proportion, whose Ornaments on each Side are equal to one Seventh of the Width in the Clear.

P L A T E XXXIV.

Another, Window whose Heighth is equal to two Widths, and one third in the Clear, and the Architrave two Ninths.

P L A T E XXXV.

A Pier in the CHINESE manner, 7 Diameters high from the lower Line of the Subplinth, to the upper Line of the Cap, which may be introduced as a Pilaster in the Front of a Building; *See the following Designs, Plates* XLI, XLII, and XLIII.

P L A T E XXXVI.

Another Pier or Pilaster, 8 Diameters and one Ninth high, from the lower Line of the Plinth to the upper Line of the Cap.

P L A T E XXXVII.

Another Pier or Pilaster, 8 Diameters and one half high from the lower Line of the Subplinth, to
the.

(5)

the upper Line of the Cap. *See Plate* XLIII, *where it is introduced as a Pilaster.*

PLATE XXXVIII.

A Garden Seat in the CHINESE manner; the Seat anfwers to the Front only, the other being diminifhed in perfpective.

PLATE XXXIX.

Another Garden Seat in the CHINESE manner, 14 Feet long, and 9 Feet 8 Inches high, proper for the Termination of a long Walk or Avenue.

PLATE XL.

Another Garden Seat in the CHINESE manner, whofe railing Receffes five Eighths of an Inch, within the outfide Frame, whofe Edge is worked with a Moulding of that Depth.

PLATE XLI.

A fmall Green Houfe in the CHINESE manner 28 Feet by 12 Feet, and 11 Feet high in the Clear.

PLATE XLII.

Another Green Houfe 27 Feet 4 Inches by 12 Feet, and 13 Feet high in the Clear.

PLATE XLIII.

Another Green Houfe 25 Feet by 12 Feet, and 15 Feet high in the Clear.

PLATE

P L A T E XLIV.

An Octagon Summer Houfe, in the CHINESE manner, 12 Feet 6 Inches Diameter, and 10 Feet from the Floor to the Foot of a Cove, which fprings 3 Feet into the Roof; this Building is moft fuitable to be placed on an Eminence which commands a good Profpect.

BOOKS

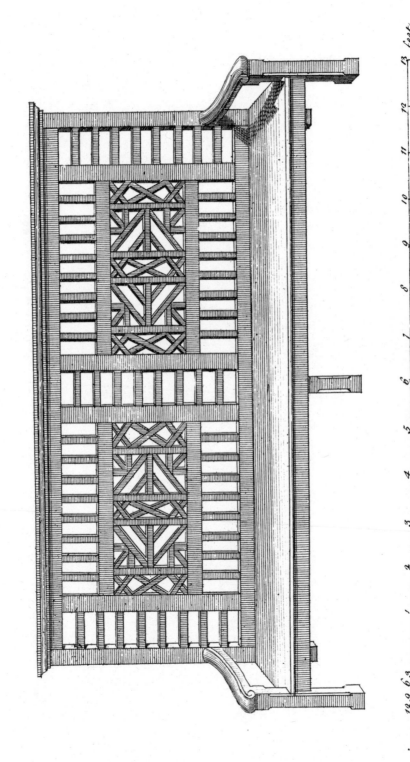

A Garden Seat in the Chinese Taste.

Parr Sculp.

inches
3 6 9 12
1 2 3 4 5 6 7 8 9 10 11 12 13 feet

Plate 39

A Garden Seat in the Chinese Taste.

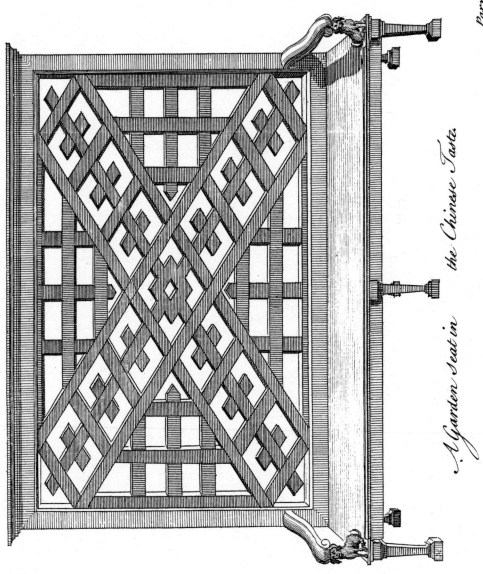

Plate 40

A Garden Seat in   the Chinese Taste.

Parr Sculp.

Plate 41

The Plan and Elevation of a   Green House in yͤ Chinese Taste

30 feet

20

10

9 8 7 6 5 4 3 2 1

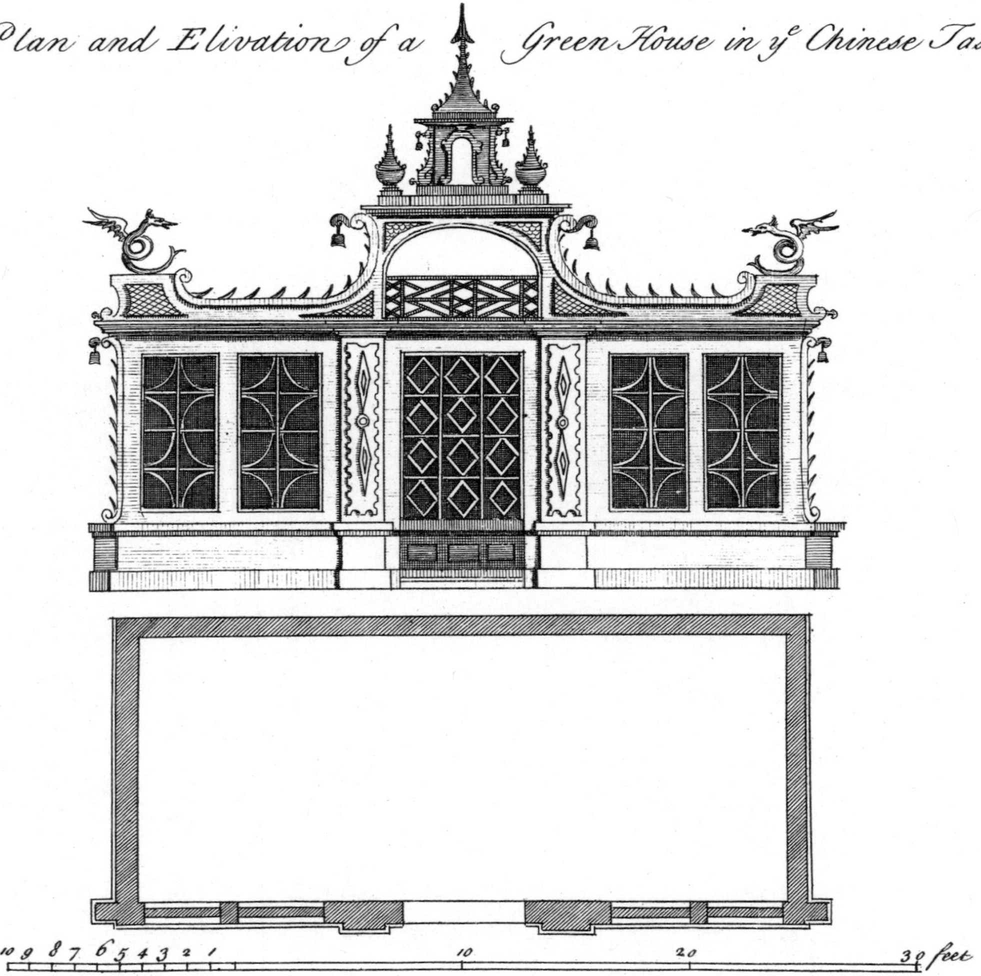

Parr Sculp.

The Plan and Elevation of a Green
House in the Chinese Taste.

Plate 42

30 feet

Parr Sculp

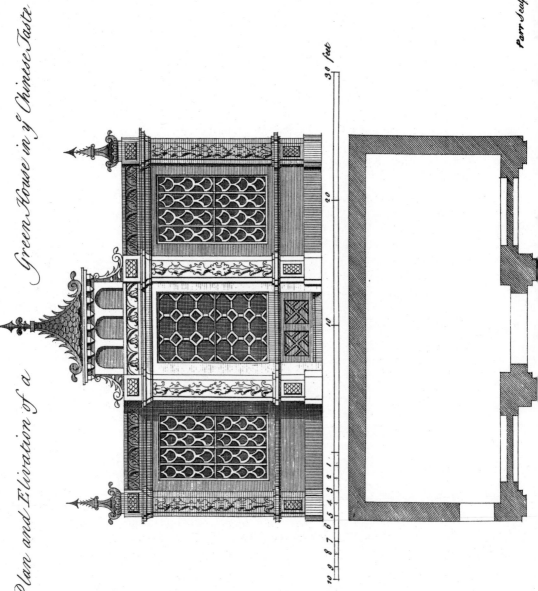

The Plan and Elevation of a   Green House in yͤ Chinese Taste.

Plate 43

Parr Sculp.

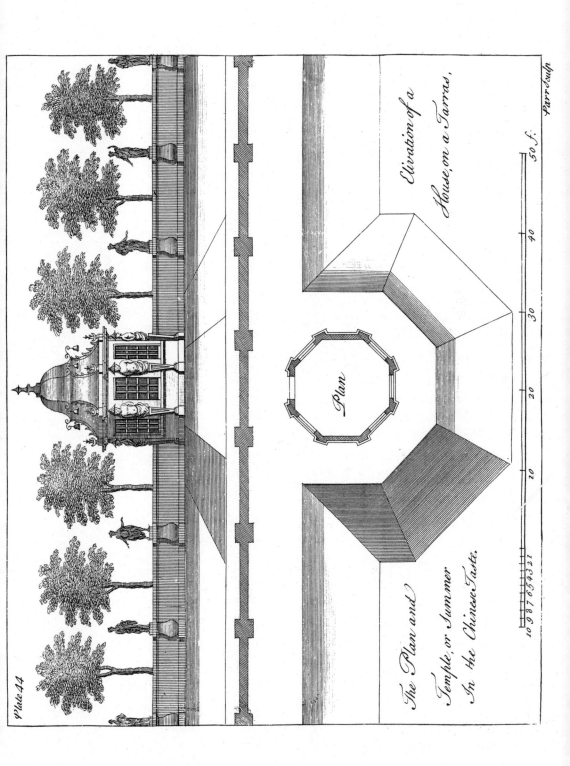

Plate 44

Plan

Elivation of a
House, on a Tarras,

The Plan and
Temple, or Summer
In the Chinese Taste.

Parr sculp.

50 f.

40

30

20

20

10 9 8 7 6 5 4 3 2 1

NEW
DESIGNS
FOR

CHINESE GATES, PALISADES, STAIR-
CASES, CHIMNEY-PIECES, CIEL-
INGS, GARDEN-SEATS, CHAIRS,
TEMPLES, &c.

ON

SIXTEEN COPPER-PLATES,

WITH

Full INSTRUCTIONS to WORKMEN.

BY

WIL. and *JOHN HALFPENNY*,
Architects,

PART IV.

Published according to Act of Parliament, January, 1752.

LONDON:

Printed for ROBERT SAYER, Map and Print-Seller, at the
Golden-Buck, opposite *Fetter-Lane, Fleet-Street.*

PART IV.

PLATE XLV.

THIS Front is decorated in the *Chinese* Manner, and is adapted to a Termini, Green-House, Pleasure Room, &c. for its Measure see the Scale.

PLATE XLVI and XLVII.

Perspective Designs for Chairs, partly in the *Chinese* Manner, most suitable for Banquetting-Houses, Rural Building, &c.

PLATE XLVIII.

Fig. 1. A Garden Seat, covered with a *Chinese* Coved Canopy, &c.

Fig 2. Two different Designs in the *Chinese* Manner, for Palisades of Wood, or Iron.

PLATE XLIX.

The Plan and Elevation of a *Chinese* Double Garden-Seat, covered with a Canopy supported by four decorated Piers.

PLATE L.

The Rails of a Stair-Case, decorated and fram'd in the *Chinese* Manner.

PLATE LI.

The Elevation of a Pair of Piers and Gates, decorated and framed in the *Chinese* Manner.

PLATE

PLATE LII.

The Plan and Elevation of an Octagon Temple, decorated in the *Chinese* Manner, with a Gallery round it, and supported by four Flights of Steps over a Piece of Water.

PLATE LIII.

The Plan and Elevation of a circular open Temple, decorated in the *Chinese* Manner.

PLATE LIV.

The Elevation of a *Chinese* Temple, with a Tarras-Walk, and Slope before it, ascended to by a Flight of Stone Steps.

PLATE LV.

The Elevation of a *Chinese* Tower or Gazebo, situated on a Rock, and raised to a considerable Heighth, and a Gallery round it to render the Prospect more compleat.

PLATES LVI, LVII, and LVIII.

Three different Designs for Chimney Pieces in the *Chinese* Taste.

PLATES LIX and LX.

Two different Cielings, decorated with Ornaments in the *Chinese* Manner.

PLATE LXI.

Fig. 20. Reprefents the Elevation and Section of a *Chinese* Roof to a Temple, or Banquetting-houfe; the Curve BC is ftruck from the
Angle A of the equilateral Triangle ABC; F is
the Frame of the Roof; G the boarded Covering, which may be painted to imitate Slates, or
Tiles, of different Shapes and Colours; H is a
Rib about two Inches and half thick, back'd
and fcrib'd down to cover the Meeting of the
Boards on the Hip; I the Cornice, which projects equal to its Height; K is the Rifing-plate,
with a fmall Lead Gutter, turned over a Fillet,
and the Horns C lapped and nailed thereon;
L is the Section of the Cove-cieling; M a Fafcia
or Margent; E are perpendicular Lines raifed
from H the Edge of the Boards, on which
the Bruffels or Thorns are fet, of an equa¹
Height.

Fig. 21. Shews the Proportions of the feveral
Moldings as at I; which I term a Pequin Cornice,
becaufe I received the firft Idea of this Ornament
from the Draught of a Temple in that City,
which I have reduced to Order as follows. Divide the Front *e e (See Fig* 20.) into 12 equal
Parts, and give one of thofe Parts to the Height
of the Cornice, and the fame to its Projection.
See Fig. 21: Divide the Height and Projection, each into 12 equal Parts, give nine to the
Height of the Horn TR, 2¼ to the Aftragal V,
and ¾ to its Fillet W, then find the Center of the
Curve R S, take TS in your Compaffes, and from
R and S defcribe the interfecting Arches at Q₂
which gives the lower Curve of the Horn SR;
through

through the fixth Divifion of Projeftion draw
the Perpendicular PD, and fet four Parts down
from f to b; having the Points TBS given,
find the Center as at P, then fet up half a Part
from b to b, and from the Points TbS find the
Center i, and defcribe the upper Curves of the
Horns; give 1¼ Part to the Projeftion of the
Aftragal V, and ¼ of a Part to its Fillet W,
the Fafcia or Margent X is 4 of fuch Parts, the
bottom Line of the finking Pannels a, ranges
with C, the Middle of $b d$, and its Curve $c g$, is
ftruck from the Center P.

Fig. 22. Is defcrib'd here to fhew the Nature
of the boarded Covering, N is Part of the Rafter ; $o o o o$ are Feather-edged Boards, not more
than 8 Inches wide, including Lap, Grove and
Tongue, but will appear in Sight no more than
6 Inches wide, when placed on the Roof, as G,
&c. one Edge is ¼ of an Inch thick, and the
other ⅜ of an Inch; there muft be but one Nail
in a Board, which will give them Room to
fhrink or fwell, to prevent their Splitting.

Fig. 23. Is placed here in a large Seal, to
fhew the Nature of the Boarding more plain.
YZ are three Boards lapped, groved, and
tongued together.

N. B. It muft be obferved in making the
Height of this Cornice $\frac{1}{12}$ of the Front, not to
ufe that Proportion any farther than a Front of
fifteen Feet, all between that and 18 Feet make
the Cornice $\frac{1}{14}$, and all from 18 to 21 Feet $\frac{1}{16}$
Part, but if it is ufed in a long Range, it muft
be fized at Difcretion, as all other Cornices are
where there are no Columns to limit their Mea-
fure.

PLATE

PLATE LXII.

Fig. 24. *Reprefents the Elevation and Section of a Roof to an open,* Chinefe *Building.*

The Curve A C is ftruck from the Angle C, of the equilateral Triangle A B C; D the per-pendicular Lines, which rife from the Extent of every Board on which the Bruffels of the Dragon are elevated; E F G H are the Curves of the Cieling, K is the Center of E F, C of FG, and I of G H; L are flender Pillars feven Inches Diameter (not diminifhed;) covered with twift-ing Ornaments, as Vines, Serpents, &c. M is the Section of the Cove-cieling, N the Mould-ing and Fafcia at the Root of the Cove; and O is the Frame of the Roof.

Fig. 25. Shews the Proportions of the feve-ral Members in the Entablature, which con-fifts of a Cornice and Fafcia; I term it a Canton Cornice, becaufe it refembles that of the great Triumphal Arch in that City, and have reduced it into Order as follows: The Heighth of this Cornice (leaving out the Horns P) is $\frac{1}{12}$ of the whole Front of the Building, and projects the fame, which are divided into 15 Parts each; give $\frac{1}{2}$ a Part to the Fillet over Q; 3 to the Fafcia Q, 7 $\frac{1}{2}$ to the great Cima-Recta R, $\frac{1}{2}$ to the Space, and 2 $\frac{1}{2}$ to the Nofe Moulding S, and one to its Fillet; add 2 of each Parts to the Horns P, and 4 to the Fafcia T, for the Projections, fee the dotted Lines; the Horns P project equal to their Height.

PLATE

PLATE LXIII.

Fig. 26. Reprefents the Elevation and Section of a *Chinefe* Octagon Ogee Roof ; A B the Cove Cieling, C the Moulding and Fafcia at the Foot of the Cove, D rifing Plate ; E Rib of the Cove, F Strut, G King-Poft, H Rafter, I a fhort Pipe under the Dragon to difcharge the Water from the Gutters, K Pillars 7 Inches Diameter, ornamented as mentioned in the foregoing Example.

Fig. 27. Shews the Proportions of a Pequin Cornice, whofe whole Height is $\frac{1}{14}$ of the Building's Diameter, which is divided into twelve equal Parts, and fubdivided ; as fhewed by the dotted Lines.

Fig. 28. Shews the Proportions of a Cove Cornice of the fame Height and Projection, and fubdivided as the dotted Lines direct.

PLATE LXIV.

Fig. 19. Reprefents the Elevation and Section of an *Indian* Roof for a Banquetting-houfe ; the Proportions are as follow : Divide the Front C D into 3 equal Parts, give one of thofe to the Height A B, and $5\frac{1}{2}$ to E O ; G the Cove-Cieling, H the Front, I the Center of the Curve K L, and M of KN ; the Soffiter P may be pannelled and ornamented at Difcretion.

F I N I S.

Pl. 45.

A Building for the Termination of a Walk
in the Chinese Taste.

10 9 8 7 6 5 4 3 2 1   10 feet

Pl. 46.

A Chair in the Chinese Taste.

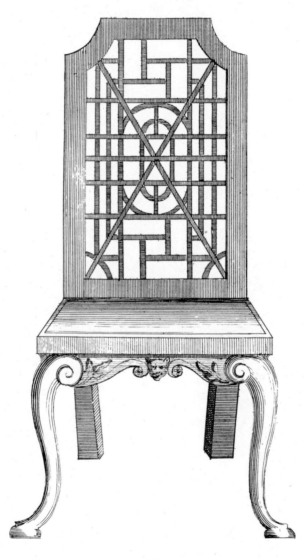

Pl.47.

A Chair in the Chinese Taste.

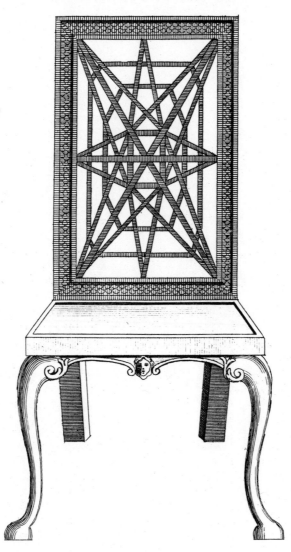

Pl. 48.

A Garden Seat in the Chinese Taste.

fig. 1.

Palisades in the Chinese Taste.

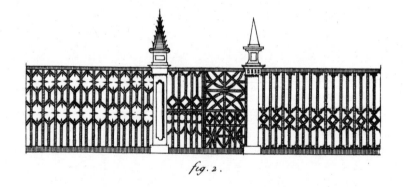

fig. 2.

Pl. 49.

A Double Garden Seat in the Chinese Taste.

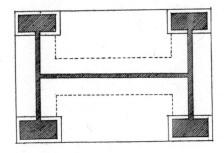

10 9 8 7 6 5 4 3 2 1   10 feet

Pl. 50.

A Stair Case in the Chinese Taste _

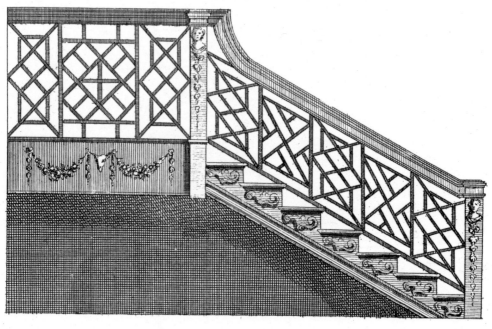

Pl. 51.

A Pair of Piers & Gate in the Chinese Taste.

10 9 8 7 6 5 4 3 2 1   10 feet

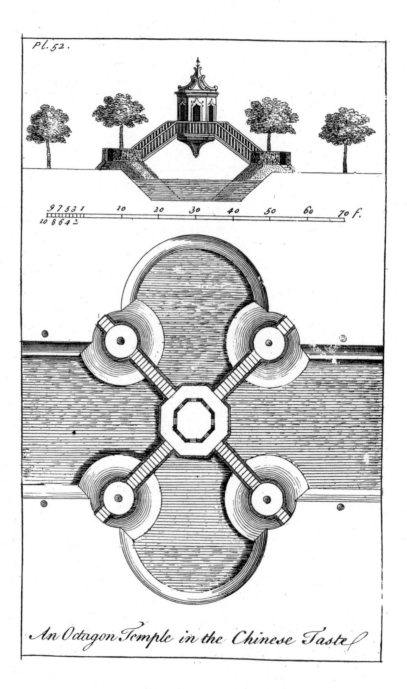

Pl. 52.

9 7 5 3 1   10   20   30   40   50   60   70 f.
10 8 6 4 2

An Octagon Temple in the Chinese Taste

Pl. 53.

A Circular open Temple in the Chinese Taste.

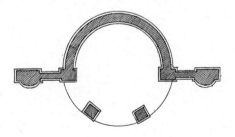

20 9 8 7 6 5 4 3 2 1   10   20 feet

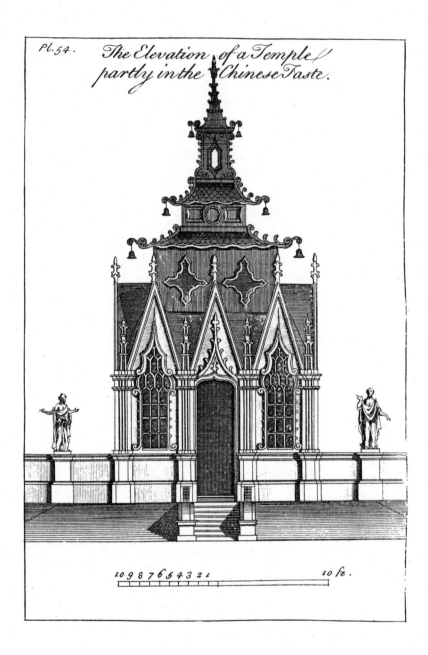

Pl.54.

The Elevation of a Temple partly in the Chinese Taste.

20 9 8 7 6 5 4 3 2 1   10 fe .

Pl. 55.

The Elevation of a Chinese Gazebo.

10 9 8 7 6 5 4 3 2 1   10   20 feet

Pl.56.

A Chimney-piece in the Chinese Taste.

Pl. 57.

A Chimney-piece in the Chinese Taste.

Pl. 58.

A Chimney-piece in the Chinese Taste

Pl.59.

A Quarter-piece for a Ceiling in the Chinese Taste.

Pl. 60.

A Quarter piece for a Ceiling in the Chinese Taste.

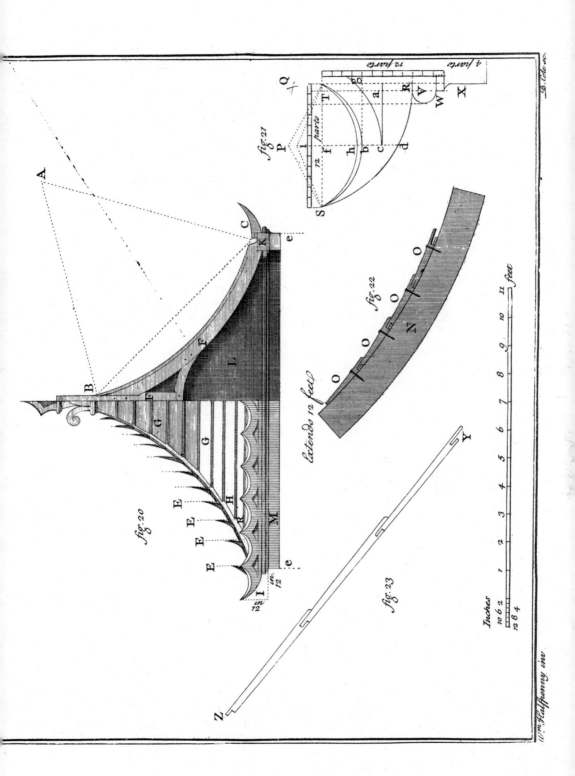

fig. 20

fig. 21

fig. 22

fig. 23

Extend⁰ 12 feet

12 parts

4 parts

12 parts

in.
12

in.
12

Inches

Feet
1 2 3 4 5 6 7 8 9 10 11

10 6 2
12 8 4

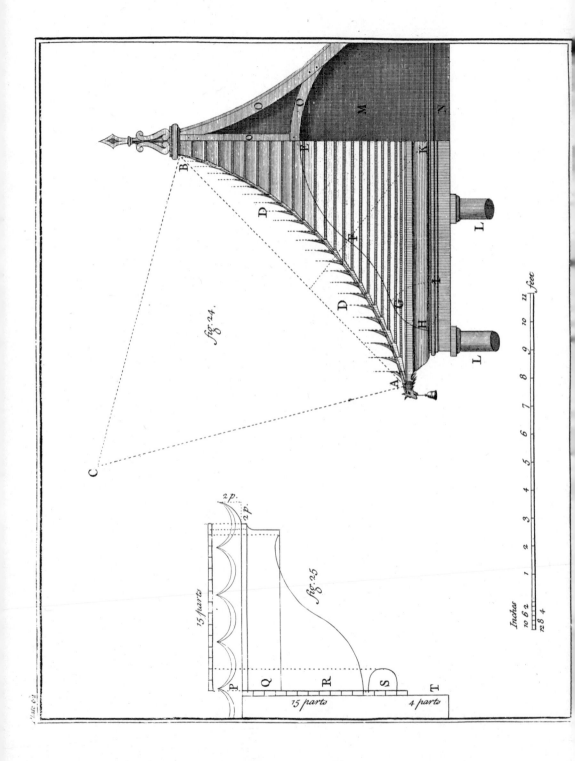

fig. 24.

fig. 25.

2 p.
2 p.

15 parts

15 parts

4 parts

Inches
10 6 2
12 8 4

feet

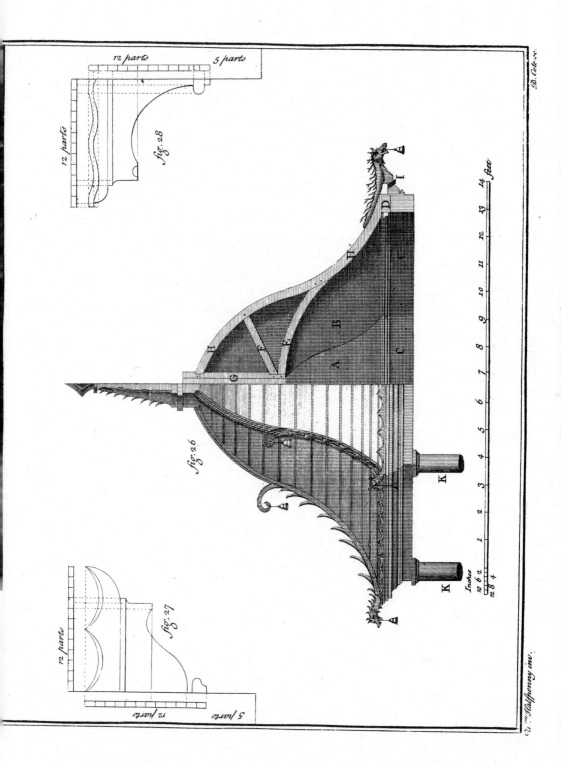

12 parts   5 parts

12 parts

Fig. 28

Fig. 26

Fig. 27

12 parts

5 parts   12 parts

G

H

A

B

C

D

E

I

K

K

L

Inches

10 6 2

12 8 4

1   2   3   4   5   6   7   8   9   10   11   12   13   14 feet

B. Cole sc.

Wm. Halfpenny inv.

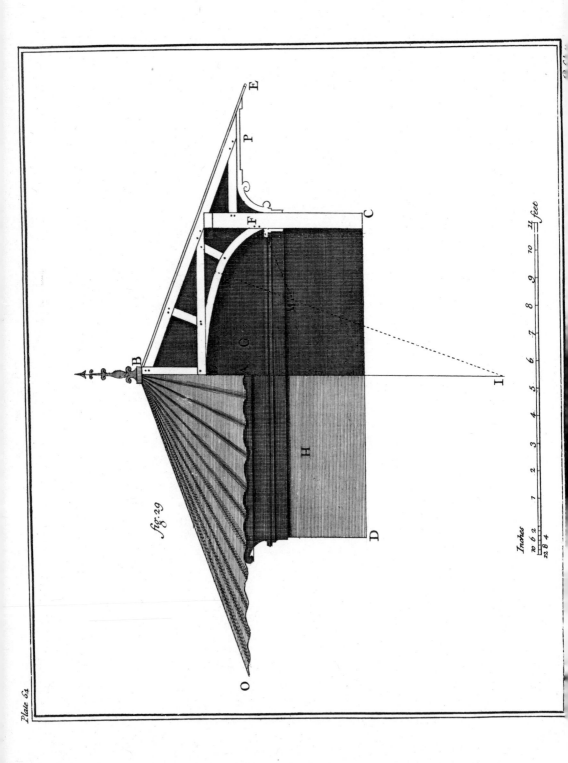

Plate 62

Fig. 29

O

E

P

F

C

B

H

D

I

Inches

Feet